ROSES

MICHAEL GIBSON

HarperCollins*Publishers*

Products mentioned in this book

Benlate* + 'Activex'	contains	benomyl
'Nimrod'-T	contains	bupirimate/triforine
'Picket'	contains	permethrin
'Rapid'	contains	pirimicarb
'Roseclear'	contains	bupirimate/pirimicarb/ triforine
'Sybol'	contains	pirimiphos-methyl
'Weedol'	contains	diquat/paraquat

Products marked thus *'Sybol'* are trade marks of Imperial Chemical Industries plc
Benlate* is a registered trade mark of Du Pont's
Read the label before you buy: use pesticides safely

Editors Maggie Daykin, Susanne Mitchell
Designer Chris Walker
Picture research Moira McIlroy

First published 1988 by
HarperCollins Publishers

This edition published 1992

© Marshall Cavendish Limited 1988, 1992

A CIP catalogue record for this book is available from the British Library.

Photoset by Bookworm Typesetting
Printed and bound in Hong Kong by Dai Nippon Printing Company

Front cover: Rose 'Peace' by Michael Warren
Back cover: Rose 'Handel' by The Harry Smith Horticultural Photographic
Collection

CONTENTS

INTRODUCTION

Rosa is a name of old and uncertain derivation, though it probably alludes to the prevailing colour of the flower. Whatever its beginnings, the rose certainly lives up to the title of 'queen of flowers'. Beloved by the early eighteenth-century painters and also appearing in many works by the Dutch masters, it is unsurpassed for its infinite variety of form, colour and fragrance, and indeed worthy of our continuing attention and cultivation.

THE ROSE FAMILIES

The rose family is really incredible. It ranges from plants no more than 15cm (6in) high through every size and shape of shrub to climbers that will top 12m (40ft). The flowers range from the five-petalled beauty and simplicity of the wild rose to the sumptuous, multi-petalled blooms of many of the old roses. Some of the latter can be up to 13cm (5in) across, while the flowers of many miniature roses are 13mm (½in) in diameter or even less. The colours cover the whole spectrum with the exception of blue, which I believe is as wide a range as that of any other plant family except possibly the iris. Small wonder that it is grown widely, too.

LEFT Hybrid tea rose 'Fragrant Cloud' is of average height, with highly scented blooms.

BELOW H.T. 'Silver Jubilee' is also a smallish grower, and an excellent variety for cutting.

Two kinds of rose are particularly well known and are to be found in most gardens, however small. These are the Hybrid Teas and the Floribundas.

Hybrid Teas (Large-flowered) Generally compact, these are upright shrubs which carry large, shapely flowers, often one to a stem but sometimes in small clusters. Heights vary between about 75cm (2½ft) and 1.2m (4ft). The well-known variety 'Peace' is an example of the taller roses but most tend to be towards the lower end of the scale, roses like 'Silver Jubilee' or 'Fragrant Cloud'. The first Hybrid Tea, 'La France', was raised in that country in 1867, so this popular group has quite a long history.

6

Floribundas (Cluster-flowered). Known before the last war as Hybrid Polyanthas, these are much more modern. Although their present form was introduced in the early 1920s, they did not really become well-known until the 1950s, when they swept the board. Because their ancestry was one of roses with little scent, they themselves are generally scentless or nearly so. In the 1950s everyone was buying them in preference to Hybrid Teas, and the impression got about that all modern roses had little fragrance. In fact there have always been, and still are, many Hybrid Teas that are sweetly scented.

Floribundas make upright shrubs in the same pattern as the Hybrid Teas, but the flowers come in clusters or trusses, sometimes with twenty or more flowers. These can be single, semi-double or fully double and just as shapely as those of the Hybrid Teas. The height range is the same for both groups, though there is one outstanding exception in 'Queen Elizabeth', which can grow to 2.4m (8ft) in a very short time. A typical Floribunda of average height is the large-flowered 'Margaret Merril' and a very good low-growing one at 60cm (2ft) is 'Wishing'.

Shrub roses can be divided, perhaps somewhat arbitrarily, into two groups: the Old Garden Roses and the Modern Shrub Roses. The dividing line came towards the end of the last century. But first of all are the wild or species roses from which all modern varieties are descended. Usually they make large shrubs – too big for a small garden – and have single flowers which appear only at midsummer or earlier. Almost all the old roses have this one flowering period of four to five weeks, the exceptions being the recurrent Bourbons, Portlands, China roses and Hybrid Perpetuals.

The once-flowering families (in historical order) are the Gallicas, Damasks, Albas, Centifolias and Moss roses. They are a very lovely but very mixed bunch and include some interesting roses such as *R. gallica* 'Officinalis', The Red Rose of Lancaster, *R.* x *alba* 'Semi-plena', The White Rose of York, and the original Cabbage Rose, *R.* x *centifolia*. Do not expect from them the shapely, high-centred blooms of the modern rose or a stiff, upright stance. Their growth is usually fairly lax, the blooms flat or cupped and simply crammed with richly-scented petals. Some of the species have

ABOVE A typical floribunda of average height is 'Margaret Merril'.

RIGHT *Rosa gallica* 'Officinalis', the Red Rose of Lancaster, is very hardy.

LEFT The modern shrub rose 'Fred Loads' is repeat-flowering and like a giant floribunda, ideally suited to the shrub or mixed border.

BELOW The dwarf shrub rose 'Ballerina' is very free flowering.

colourful hips as well, once the flowers have gone.

Modern shrub roses are mostly repeat-flowering and the group includes the Rugosa family typified by wine-red 'Roseraie de l'Hay' and the Hybrid Musks – of which pink 'Felicia' is a good example. A number of them, such as 'Fred Loads' and 'Chinatown', are in fact simply giant Floribundas, too large to be used in bedding, but once again they are a very diverse group and include dwarf types like 'Ballerina' with its appleblossom blooms.

Climbers It would be as well first of all to distinguish between a climber and a rambler. In general terms (though there are exceptions) a climber has quite large flowers in small clusters and most modern ones are recurrent. It forms a permanent framework of shoots. A rambler sends up new, flexible shoots from the base each year and is more easily trained. It will not have a second flowering but carries its quite small blooms in generously large clusters.

Climbing sports are climbing versions of bush roses which, though they will carry exactly the same flowers as the bush version, may not be nearly as recurrent. If a rose has the letters Cl. or the word Climbing in front of it in a catalogue, it will be a sport. For example, 'Climbing Iceberg' – which happens to be one of the best and fully recurrent – is a sport of the Floribunda 'Iceberg'.

One or two roses come half-way in between a rambler and a climber, which can be rather confusing. The early-flowering and very lovely 'Albertine' is an example. It has fairly large flowers in small clusters and stiff, strong canes, but is once-flowering only. By tradition it was called a rambler but now it is more usually classed as a climber.

Miniature roses are just what the name implies, miniature replicas of their larger cousins, the smallest no more than 15cm (6in) high. Their origin was in a small rose from China with pink flowers and all the early ones were white or pink. Crossing them with Floribundas brought many other colours into the range and also increased the size of the bushes. Modern miniatures are often 30–38cm (12–15in) in height and some have flowers which I consider too big for the plant. It is sometimes thought that miniatures, because of their size and delicate, airy growth, are not as hardy as full-size roses. Understandable, but in general this is not the case.

Ground cover roses The development of these is comparatively recent, though there have been a few so-called ground cover roses for some time. Most of these, like *R.* x *paulii*, are simply sprawling, widespreading growers which cover a lot of ground but may be up to 1.2m (4ft) tall, which is not my idea of a ground cover plant. The really prostrate ground cover roses have largely been developed from ramblers such as *R. wichuraiana*, which will grow along the ground, rooting as it goes. 'Max Graf' was the first, but the more modern 'Grouse' and 'Pheasant' give a much more dense coverage. Among the miniatures, 'Snow Carpet' is very effective with a spread of about 90cm (3ft).

ABOVE *Rosa wichuraiana*, which has been used in the development of many of the prostrate ground cover roses. This rose itself makes good ground cover.

LEFT 'Max Graf' is one of the earlier varieties of ground cover rose, and a vigorous rugosa hybrid.

THE ROSE IN THE GARDEN

Hybrid Teas and Floribundas have been traditionally used for bedding, for which they are very suitable as each variety grows to a more or less uniform height and they are in flower over a very long period. Floribundas are perhaps the most suitable of all as they usually repeat much more quickly than Hybrid Teas and there are far more blooms per plant.

Hybrid teas and floribundas are traditionally grown in their own beds or borders and ideally should be planted in bold groups of each variety to avoid a 'spotty' effect. There is a trend now towards growing other plants with roses.

Whether or not varieties should be mixed must remain a matter of personal choice, but to avoid a rather spotty effect (for all varieties do not flower at exactly the same time) plant each variety in clumps of four or five plants.

Bear in mind, too, the blending of colours and do not put a cerise pink rose like 'Wendy Cussons' next to a bright scarlet variety such as 'Summer Holiday'. Pastel shades make good dividers between colours that might clash. Also, check ultimate heights to avoid putting a rose like 'Alexander' in the same bed as, say, 'Dutch Gold'. The first will reach 1.2m (4ft) while the latter stays at 75cm (2½ft).

Rose hedges Some of the taller Floribundas and Hybrid Teas are very suitable for hedges. 'Alexander' is one, and varieties such as 'Anne Harkness', 'Southampton' and that old favourite 'Peace' are others. For a really tall hedge 'Queen Elizabeth' is the rose to choose, but with all these varieties stagger the planting if they are to form a screen.

A much denser hedge will be the result if some of the shrub roses are used, and many of them also grow a good deal taller. There are ideal varieties in the Rugosa family, all of which have fine disease-proof foliage right down to the ground. They carry flowers all through the summer and autumn, to be followed in some cases by ornamental hips. Perhaps the best are 'Roseraie de l'Hay' with wine-red double flowers but no hips, or the rather shorter 1.2m (4ft) 'Frau Dagmar Hartopp' with soft pink flowers and hips too.

The Hybrid Musk roses such as 'Felicia' and 'Penelope' also make good hedges but may need a certain amount of restraint by training them on wires strung between uprights; otherwise they can take up a lot of room. Both Rugosas and Hybrid Musks are shrub roses which, as a class, look very good in groups on their own or mixed with other shrubs. The Rugosas and Musks are recurrent, but many of the others which are not, such as *R.* x *alba* 'Maxima', have most attractive grey-green leaves. Many species roses also have lovely ferny foliage and are admirable for specimen planting, perhaps in a lawn or to form a focal point in the garden.

The rugosa rose, 'Frau Dagmar Hartopp', makes an excellent hedge. Attractive hips follow the flowers.

The hybrid musk roses, like 'Penelope', also make good hedges but may need a certain amount of restraint by training them on wires strung between posts, otherwise they can take up a lot of room. Hybrid musks are beautifully scented and recurrent flowering.

LEFT Arches and pergolas make excellent supports for climbers and ramblers and the plants benefit from the good air circulation around them. Choose varieties of moderate vigour.

BELOW Climbing rose 'Golden Showers' is ideal for growing on walls and other supports such as arches and pergolas.

Focal points can again be formed by standard roses, particularly by the weeping standards, in which the head is formed from one of the ramblers and the long, flexible canes hang (or 'weep') right down to the ground, covered from top to bottom with blooms. Ordinary standards are useful for giving height (the change of level which delights the eye in the garden) to a planting of bedding roses, perhaps as a row down the centre of a long bed or as a single standard in the centre of a round or square bed.

The colour can be chosen to complement or to contrast with that of the other roses. There are half and quarter standards as well as those of full height and, if they are banked one behind the other (with the shortest or perhaps bush roses at the front) this can be very striking indeed, particularly if there is a mellow brick wall as a background.

Climbers and ramblers Perhaps the most usual way to grow these is on walls though, as mentioned in the section on Training, it is best to keep ramblers to an openwork support such as a trellis, arch, pergola or pillar. For the latter many of the modern climbers, such as 'Golden Showers', which are of only moderate vigour – up to about 2.4m (8ft) – are ideal. A really rampant grower like 'Mermaid' would overwhelm a pillar in no time.

Growing some of the more vigorous climbers and ramblers up trees will create a sight you will never forget as the swags of bloom cascade down from the branches. But do make sure that you use a tree of sufficient size and, above all, strength. The weight and wind resistance of some of the best tree-climbing roses like 'Wedding Day', 'Rambling Rector' or 'Bobby James' would bring down a small or rotten tree in no time.

Miniature roses Many people think these are house plants because they are often sold in pots. However, they are quite at home in the garden and can be used on rockeries or for edging beds of roses or other plants, provided they are not in shade. They are also admirable for use in tubs and troughs if adequately watered at all times. The troughs raise them up above ground level, where it is easier to appreciate the beauty of their tiny blooms. The same applies if they are planted round the edge of a sunken garden or in a massed planting in terraced beds.

I have from time to time seen attempts at creating a miniature rose garden, complete with grass paths between the beds, but this is rarely successful. If the width of the paths is to scale it is almost impossible to cut the grass, and somehow the different varieties do not blend as they do in full size bedding schemes. It is difficult to explain just what the problem is, but somehow it never does look right.

If miniature roses are grown in raised beds or borders they will be much nearer the eye so one can then more easily appreciate their qualities, such as perfectly-shaped flowers and foliage.

BUYING ROSES

The only really safe way of making sure that the rose you would like to buy is what you really want is to see it growing somewhere first, preferably over quite a long period. Only in this way can you judge how well it will stand up to rough weather, how continuously it is in flower, whether it sheds its petals cleanly when the flowers die, how tall and bushy it will grow and whether it holds its colour well in bright sunlight.

Some nurseries have display gardens in which they grow the roses they sell, as opposed to the nursery fields, in which the roses will be in their first year and so will not have reached their full size. This last point is of particular importance when choosing shrub roses as it is very difficult to visualize just how big some of them will become.

Buying from a catalogue can be quite satisfactory if you go to a reputable firm, but remember that colour printing has not yet reached a stage where it can be relied on to match the delicate tones found in some roses. And the reds are particularly unreliable. In addition, nursery catalogues do not as a rule mention if a rose is prone to mildew or blackspot. This is because a variety's susceptibility to disease can vary widely from one part of the country to another or even from one garden to another but if you have seen them growing locally you will have a good idea.

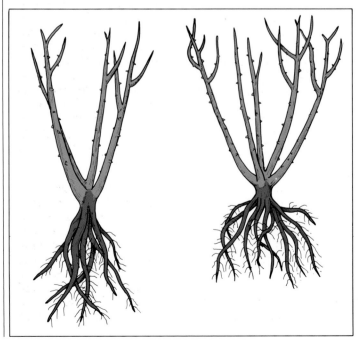

Hybrid teas, floribundas and shrub roses should have a good, fibrous root system and a minimum of two strong shoots, firm and unwrinkled, and of pencil thickness.

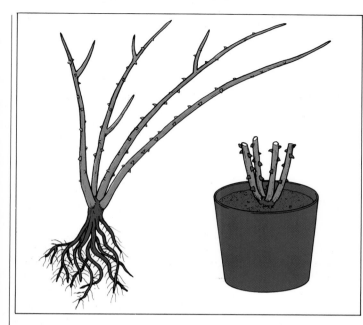

FAR LEFT Climbers and ramblers should have similar qualities to bush roses, but the shoots should have been left much longer – about 45cm (1½ft). There should be at least two, and ideally three or four.

LEFT When buying container-grown roses, check that the plant is properly established.

Buying the best From whatever source you buy your roses they should fulfil certain conditions:

- Hybrid Teas, Floribundas and shrub roses should have a good, fibrous root system and a *minimum* of two strong shoots, firm and unwrinkled, and of pencil thickness at least. Three or four shoots is the ideal.
- For climbers, the same applies but the shoots should have been left much longer, say, approximately 45cm (1½ft).
- The standard roses should be double-budded; that is, the shoots at the top of the stem should be sprouting out from two different places.

Any roses not reaching these standards are not entitled to be described as first grade plants.

Buying container-grown roses has the great advantage that they can be planted at almost any time.

However, make sure by asking whether the roses really have been container grown and are not just unsold (and possibly inferior) stock from the previous season with most of their root growth chopped off so that they can be stuffed into a container. This is, regrettably, not unknown, but a covering of moss on the container soil or roots coming out at the bottom are indications that the rose is properly established. As a general rule, if in any doubt – don't buy!

Buying prepacked roses in a store or supermarket may be satisfactory provided they have not been stored in the wrong conditions for some time. If they look dried up and wrinkled or if white, worm-like shoots have started to grow they really should be avoided and the proportion of these second grade plants is usually higher than it should be.

SITE, SOIL AND PLANTING

Roses will grow happily in almost any position provided they have full sun for the greater part of the day. They will also grow in most soils, but the ideal is a good medium loam that is moisture retentive but well drained and slightly acid – about 6.5 on the pH scale. It is a myth that they actually prefer clay, though they will grow happily in clay that does not become waterlogged.

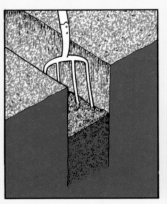

Double digging: dig the bottom of each trench; mix in manure.

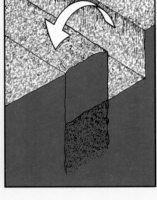

Take out next trench and throw soil forward into the first trench.

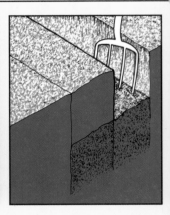

Again dig bottom to full depth of the fork and continue in this way.

The soil If your soil is heavy and you are doubtful about the drainage, double digging may be necessary, incorporating plenty of peat and compost as you turn the soil over. A clay soil can be improved by adding calcium sulphate at 1.4kg sq m (3lb sq yd). Nitrochalk will reduce acidity. Peat and leafmould will increase it. A soil testing kit will eliminate guesswork.

Your roses will be in place a long time and give you years of pleasure, so take trouble with their new home. Carry out any digging necessary two to three months before you intend to plant so that the soil can settle down again and bacteria can begin the work of breaking down the organic matter you may have incorporated.

Planting All of the above preparation applies if you are planting up a new rose bed. Don't try to plant new roses in a bed that has grown roses for a number of years as the ground will have become what is known as 'rose sick' and they will never flourish. The soil must be either changed or sterilized, neither of which is a task the average gardener will welcome. Individual roses in an established bed may be replaced by digging out a hole about 45cm (1½ft) across and deep and putting new soil in along with the newly planted rose.

The ideal month for planting is November, though for bare-root roses it can take place at any time while they are dormant and provided it is not frosty or the ground waterlogged. The container-grown roses can be planted out at almost any time.

Inspect your roses when you have unwrapped them. Cut away any dead or diseased growth. Shorten long, thick roots by about one-third to encourage fine feeding roots to develop from them. If the plants look dry, put them in a bucket of water for an hour or two. If you cannot plant straight away, heel the roses in in a trench.

How far apart you plant depends on the size and habit of the roses. This you will have been able to establish if you have seen them growing at the nursery or in other gardens. About 60cm (2ft) apart is a good average for bedding roses. Make the holes wide enough for the roots to spread out evenly and deep enough so that the crown or budding union of each plant is just below the soil level. A cane laid across the hole will help you to judge the depth accurately.

Prepare a planting mixture of half and half soil and 'Forest Bark' Ground and Composted Bark or peat, adding a slow-release fertilizer such as Rose 'Plus' or bonemeal. This can be placed round the roots of the rose when you have placed it in the hole and will get it away to a good start. Fill in the rest of the hole with soil and tread firmly but not too hard. Water well. Roses planted in spring should be pruned at the time of planting.

Sometimes you will find a rose has all its roots pointing in one direction and it is impossible to spread them properly. Put the rose in at the side of the hole rather than at the centre and fan the roots out as far as possible. The same applies with a climber, though for a different reason. As the soil near a wall is likely to be very dry, climbers should be planted at least 45cm (1½ft) away from the wall surface and the roots fanned out away from it towards damper soil. Do not tie climbers in to their horizontal training wires until they have settled in the soil.

 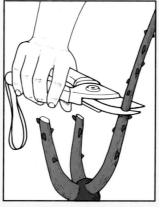

Before planting roses inspect them carefully and if necessary cut away any dead or diseased growth. Shorten long, thick roots by about one-third to encourage fine feeding roots to develop.

17

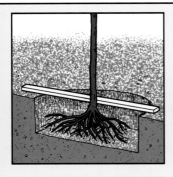

Planting a standard rose: plant just deep enough to cover the roots; this will discourage suckers. The stake should be inserted before the roots are covered with soil, to prevent root damage. Some fine soil should be worked well between the roots. The soil should then be firmed really thoroughly.

When planting standard roses, which will always need a stake to support them, put the stake into the hole first. If driven in last, it could damage the rose roots. Plant standards just deep enough to cover the roots; this will discourage suckers from the rather sucker-prone Rugosa rootstock that is used for these roses.

Aftercare Once the roses are growing away happily their welfare should not be forgotten. At least twice during the growing period – after pruning and again early in July – a small handful per plant of a special rose fertilizer such as Rose 'Plus' should be sprinkled round each plant and gently hoed in. Do not put fertilizer on after the end of July as it would encourage late growth which would not have time to ripen before frosts killed it off.

Some time in April, after the soil has begun to warm up a little, it is a good idea to apply a mulch to the rose beds. This is a layer of preferably organic material some 7.5–10cm (3–4in) thick spread over the beds to smother weeds, prevent the evaporation of moisture, and keep the soil temperature fairly even. Well rotted stable manure is the ideal as it provides a lot of rose food as well as carrying out the other functions of a mulch, but it is not always easy to get. Compost provides food, too, but can look unsightly. 'Forest Bark' Ground and Composted Bark and peat make excellent mulches but do not provide food. If you do not mulch, keep the weeds down by hoeing or with 'Weedol', carefully applied.

TRAINING CLIMBERS

We have dealt with the planting of climbing roses against walls and mentioned the horizontal wires along which they should be trained. The reason for these horizontal wires is that if a climber were just allowed to have its head it would grow upwards but it would not spread out much sideways to cover the wall and all the flowers would be at the top.

Horizontal training As long as the main shoots are allowed to grow unrestricted, a chemical inhibitor present in the plant prevents the lower buds which would produce side shoots from breaking into life. If, however, the shoots are fanned out and trained along horizontal wires, the inhibitor ceases to function and flowering side shoots will appear at all levels. Some of these are tied in at the next wire up the wall so that the rose will gradually spread out not only sideways but also upwards in a controlled fashion.

Strong, galvanized iron wire is the best to use and it will last for many years. It should be strung between vine eyes, the strands about 45cm (1½ft) apart and about 7.5cm (3in) from the wall surface. If there is any difficulty in driving the vine eyes into the mortar between the bricks, drill holes first, fractionally larger than the small ends of the vine eyes. Tie the rose shoots to the outside of the wires as this will make pruning much easier later on.

Ramblers Talking of tangled growth reminds one inevitably of ramblers, but it is perhaps more by pruning (dealt with elsewhere) than training that one keeps their otherwise undisciplined growth in check. Training does come into it, of course, but it is as well to keep ramblers away from walls. Most are prone to mildew and there is likely to be a lack of air circulation near a wall which will only make the problem

The stems of climbers should be trained horizontally to encourage plenty of flowering side shoots to develop

worse. Grow them on an openwork fence, on pillars, tripods, arches or pergolas, while the more vigorous ones can be grown up healthy trees.

On a fence, fan out the shoots in the same way, but if you are growing a climber or a rambler up a pillar on its own, or one that supports a pergola, this would be difficult. Instead, train it in a spiral round the support to allow flowering side shoots to form. With less vigorous modern climbers like 'Golden Showers' which have fairly stiff canes, make sure this training is started early on – before the shoots have become hard and inflexible.

PRUNING

There is considerable difference of opinion, even among the experts, as to which is the best time to prune. The reason for this is quite simple. You can prune at almost any time when the roses are dormant or nearly so. However, it should not be thought that there are no rules governing when pruning should be done.

When pruning a bush rose such as a hybrid tea or floribunda, first open up the centre of the bush and remove dead and weak growth. Then reduce remaining strong stems, pruning harder for hybrid teas than for floribundas.

Newly-cut shoots will be likely to die back if frost gets at them, so do not prune in the middle of a frosty spell, however long it may last. Use your judgement, as you have to do in many other aspects of gardening, and you should not go far wrong. March in the south and April in the north of the country are the traditional months, so use this as your guide. The plants will then be stirring into life and the buds beginning to break into leaf, which is the ideal in many ways.

However, it is perfectly all right to prune when the bushes are fully dormant as gardeners who prune in the autumn or early winter do. The drawback is that one is to an extent gambling with the weather, and if the winter turns out to be exceptionally cold the bushes will probably have to be gone over again in the spring to remove shoots that have died back. It can even mean cutting almost to ground level but, in most winters, in the south at any rate, autumn pruning can be safely undertaken at a time when there are not so many jobs to do in the garden as there are in the early months of the year.

When a shoot has died back it

will look shrivelled and be light brown. Dieback can spread quite rapidly down a shoot, attacking the central, pithy part first. If a shoot reveals a brown centre when it is cut into during pruning the dieback is at an early stage and one can probably halt it by cutting to the next bud down the stem and continuing like this until clean white wood is reached. At all times, however, dead wood should be removed completely.

Why prune? Quite simply to encourage strong new shoots, which are the ones that will carry the best and largest flowers. If left to themselves, rose shoots would gradually deteriorate and over a number of years new ones would take their place. Pruning accelerates this natural process and it also performs other useful functions. It gets rid of dead, diseased and spindly shoots which would not bear worthwhile flowers. Any shoots much less than pencil thickness are best dispensed with and if the centre of a bush looks congested some thinning out is recommended to improve air circulation. If two shoots are rubbing together or look as if they might do so eventually, one of them should be removed or at least cut back.

Finally, when pruning one should try to end up with a reasonably balanced bush. This does not perhaps matter so much in a massed bedding scheme as a lack of balance may well be hidden, but it is very important with a rose grown as a specimen shrub.

When pruning, it can be difficult to see the buds, as they form in the leaf axil, the angle between leaf stem and branch (see left). Always cut above an outward-pointing bud.

Dead and diseased shoots must be cut out completely, right back to healthy tissue. Always use really sharp secateurs to ensure clean cuts and no bruising of the stems.

How to prune Though some professionals use pruning knives, most people find secateurs easier to handle. Make sure, however, that you have a really good pair, even if they seem relatively expensive. Cheap secateurs may distort so that they do not make a clean cut, and badly designed ones will bruise the rose stems. Both these faults will encourage the entry of disease spores.

If you have really good secateurs and keep them clean and sharp at all times, they should last you a lifetime. Clean and disinfect the blades with a rag dipped in methylated spirits if you have been using them on diseased wood.

Your pruning cut should be made about 19mm (¾in) above a bud and slope down at an angle of approximately 45° away from it.

Cutting to a bud that faces outwards will encourage spreading growth, but do not be too worried if you cannot find one at the right place. Roses do not always follow the rules we make for them and it is quite likely that a bud lower down will take over and make the stronger shoot. Just cut to encourage shoots in the direction you would like them to go and hope for the best!

Pruning different rose groups

Hybrid Teas Once dead and diseased wood has been removed and the centre of the bush opened up if it needs it, the remaining main shoots should be cut back to about 15–20cm (6–8in), that is, to the nearest bud. The main aim of pruning is to make the plant as shapely as you can.

Floribunda roses Follow exactly the same sequence but the main shoots can be left rather longer – about 25–30cm (10–12in) – and the side shoots shortened by about two-thirds. Lighter pruning is used here because with Floribundas the size of the individual flowers is not so all-important as it is with Hybrid Teas. It is the quantity of flowers that counts when the plant produces such a mass display.

Climbers Apart from the fact that they can be difficult to reach, these are comparatively simple to prune. As a rule, all that is needed is the shortening of the side shoots by about two-thirds, and this should be done in autumn. The main canes should not be touched unless they are exceeding their allotted space, in which case they can be shortened. If the rose is becoming bare at the base, one of them can be cut back really hard to encourage new growth lower down.

After flowering (which means late summer) the ideal treatment for ramblers is to cut out completely the shoots that have flowered and in their place to tie in the new shoots that have formed that year. If insufficient new shoots have formed, some of the old ones can be left, but their side shoots should be shortened. They will flower quite well, though not as profusely as the new ones.

Shrub roses Some people hold that shrub roses need no pruning but there seems little doubt that they do flower better with a little attention – say the cutting back of their side shoots by about two-thirds – and the removal of any dead or diseased wood. The latter can be

ABOVE Climbers are pruned by shortening the side shoots in the autumn.

BELOW 'New Dawn' is a climber that should be pruned regularly.

cut out at any time as it should be with the wild or species roses, which require no other attention.

Miniature roses Repeat the pattern outlined for Floribundas, reducing the overall height by about two-thirds. Some, like 'Baby Masquerade', tend to have a particularly twiggy form and are certain to need a good thinning out.

To enjoy your roses at their peak of performance, they will demand of you a fair amount of attention. But much of the work involved is simply done and the rewards are enormous.

When flowers have faded cut back the shoots to a bud at least 10–13cm (4–5in) below the spent flowers. This will encourage more flowers to follow.

Deadheading If you remove the hips that start to form once a flower has faded, more flowers will be produced. In other words, the rose is carrying out its natural cycle of reproduction by producing hips or seed pods, and if these are not allowed to develop by deadheading the plant will try again. Do not, however, simply pull the dead flowers off. You will be left with unsightly flower stalks which will die back. Also, a new shoot is likely to form very high up the stem and will be much weaker and more spindly than one from lower down. So cut the shoot to a bud at least 10–13cm (4–5in) below the spent flower. With Floribundas, cut to the first or second bud below a flower truss.

Suckers All the roses we buy from a nursery are grown on the roots of wild roses of various kinds, which gives them extra vigour and other desirable qualities. A sucker is a shoot coming from these roots (the rootstock) rather than from the cultivated variety. If left to grow, such will be its vigour that over a number of years, it will gradually take over and the cultivated variety that was budded on to it will die.

It is often said that one can recognize a sucker because each leaf will have seven leaflets. This is quite a good guide but not infallible. However, the stems and thorns are also likely to show differences, often being a much paler green. If you *are* in doubt as to whether a shoot is a sucker, trace it back to its source (using a trowel if necessary) and if it comes from below the budding union it is a sucker. Pull it away from the root. Alternatively, spray with a touch of 'Weedol'. Cutting a sucker would be the equivalent of pruning it, that is, you would encourage it to grow more strongly.

Shoots appearing on the stems of standard roses below the head are, in fact, suckers, as the stem is part of the rootstock. They should be snapped off as soon as seen.

Disbudding A number of Hybrid Tea varieties have clusters of perhaps four to five buds on a single stem. Sometimes, as with roses such as 'Pink Favourite', they are so close together that the flowers may not be able to open properly. And even if they can open, the more flowers there are the smaller they will be. If some, or all, of the side buds are pinched out as soon as they are large enough to be handled, much larger and better blooms will result.

Autumn pruning or cut-back Some of the taller-growing Hybrid Teas and Floribundas can be damaged by strong winter winds. Shoots can be whipped about, their thorns tearing the bark of others and encouraging the entry of disease. And in heavy, easily compacted soils a small funnel may be formed in the earth at the point where the shoots emerge. If water collects in this and freezes, it may damage the crown of the plant when it thaws. So some time towards the end of October cut back the taller roses by one-third.

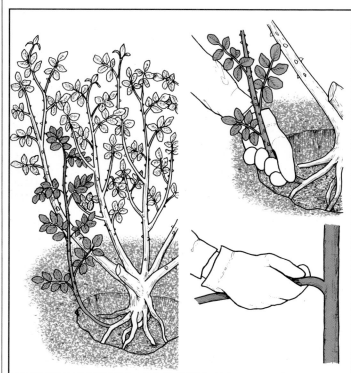

Suckers grow from the roots of bush roses such as hybrid teas and floribundas. They should be removed by digging the soil away and then wrenching them out. Shoots on the stems of standards are also suckers and should be snapped off as soon as they are seen.

ENEMIES OF THE ROSE

Like most other plants, the rose has its share of enemies, some more easily dealt with than others. However, a watchful eye and speedy action at the first signs of trouble should prevent any serious damage or loss of prized plants. Here are some guidelines.

ABOVE Greenfly multiply quickly.

ABOVE RIGHT First signs of rust.

RIGHT Damage by leaf-rolling sawfly.

Insect pests Quite a large number of insects will attack roses but comparatively few cause serious problems. The majority can be dealt with at one and the same time by spraying with a good insecticide such as 'Sybol'. This enters and moves in the plant tissue so that it does not get washed off by rain and will last for a number of weeks. The pests most likely to worry the average gardener are:

Greenfly Small green or sometimes pinky-brown insects that cluster on new shoots, flower buds and under leaves, sucking the sap and distorting growth. Remove with finger and thumb if only a few present. Otherwise, spray with 'Sybol', or 'Rapid', which does not affect welcome visitors, such as bees or ladybirds.

Caterpillars These eat holes in the leaves. Spray with 'Picket' or pick off by hand if only a few.

Leaf-rolling sawfly An increasing problem. A small fly which lays its eggs in the leaf margins, causing them to roll up lengthways, thus protecting the grub when it hatches. Spray with 'Sybol' at the end of April and again early in May. Pick off and burn affected leaves.

26

Diseases The diseases that attack roses are generally more serious than insect problems, but nowadays they can be contained. They are:

Blackspot Black spots with fringed edges on the leaves, which rapidly grow in size until the leaf yellows and drops off. The plant can become defoliated and weakened. Spray at once with Benlate + 'Activex' or 'Nimrod'-T. Alternatively, use a combined fungicide and greenfly killer such as 'Roseclear' if both pest and disease are present.

Mildew Mildew is a greyish, powdery deposit on leaves and flower stems which can spread rapidly to the whole plant and distort growth. It is at all times unsightly and should be sprayed at once as for Blackspot.

Rose rust Serious, as it will spread rapidly from plant to plant and can be a killer. Fortunately, it attacks only certain varieties and is found only in certain areas, more especially in the eastern counties. Orange spots on the undersides of the leaves are the first sign. These later turn black. Spraying with 'Nimrod'-T should give some control; a prevention rather than a cure.

Now for a few general tips on the subject of spraying.

● Always follow the instructions on the bottle or packet. Doubling the dose of something will not double its effectiveness and may cause harm, so do not experiment.
● Do not spray in hot sunshine or you risk leaf-scorch. Early evening is a good time.
● Do not spray when it is windy. Fine spray can be carried many yards and may blow into your face or get on to other plants where bees are active.
● Store all chemical concentrates in a safe, dry place well away from children and pets.

ABOVE Mildew spreads rapidly and severely distorts growth.

RIGHT Blackspot can cause defoliation and weakens growth, so act quickly.

SIXTY OF THE BEST

The following notes describe some of the best roses in the various rose families dealt with earlier in this book. However, I think that it is worth repeating once again that the best way to choose your roses is first to see them growing in a local garden. Words and even pictures can seldom do justice to their beauty. All these varieties should be easily available from garden centres or from specialist nurseries.

Hybrid tea rose 'Alexander' is a tall grower.

HYBRID TEAS

'Alec's Red' One of the best scarlet roses for bedding, holding its colour well in all weathers. The scent is outstanding and the blooms come with great freedom and a quick repeat. Upright growth to 75cm (2½ft) with healthy, mid-green, glossy leaves. RNRS Gold Medal and medal for fragrance.

'Alexander' A handsome rose which, as it will reach 1.2m (4ft), can be grown as a specimen shrub or used in a large bed. It will also make a fine low hedge as it bushes out quite well and has a good covering of healthy deep green, semi-glossy leaves. The slightly fragrant flowers, which come with great freedom, are a deep, rich vermilion. RNRS Certificate of Merit.

'Alpine Sunset', a hybrid tea.

'Alpine Sunset' One of the best roses of recent years, with large, shapely, sweetly-scented flowers in blends of golden yellow and peach-pink. They come singly or two or three to a stem with considerable freedom. A vigorous grower to 75cm (2½ft) with healthy, glossy leaves. RNRS Trial Ground Certificate.

'Blessings' Dating back to 1968, 'Blessings' is still unsurpassed as a bedding rose that is never out of bloom. Its beautiful coral-pink deepens towards the centre of the large, fairly loosely-formed flowers, which are sweetly scented. Of average height, 75cm (2½ft), the vigorous bushes have semi-glossy leaves more healthy than most roses of this colour. RNRS Certificate of Merit.

'Camphill Glory' Very shapely flowers, creamy pink with deeper pink flushes, which stand rain remarkably well considering the number of petals. Free-flowering and tall at 1m (3½ft). Mid-green foliage.

'Dutch Gold' Shapely, bright yellow blooms that hold their colour well and are very fragrant. Some flowers may be of exhibition size and standard, but there may be split blooms, too. Upright growth to medium height. Gold Medal in The Hague.

'Fragrant Cloud' Regrettably, not as healthy as it once was, but still well worth growing for its non-stop show of large, bright geranium-red blooms which are among the most sweetly scented of all roses. Of average height and bushing out well, it has dark, glossy leaves. RNRS Gold Medal and RHS Award of Merit.

'Grandpa Dickson' Not a rose for poor, sandy soils, but otherwise a variety with shapely yellow flowers that are just as much at home in the garden as they are on the show bench. In other words, rainproof but not much scent. A short, upright grower, needing closer planting than usual. Three Gold Medals and an RHS Award of Merit.

Hybrid tea 'Grandpa Dickson' has rainproof blooms.

'Just Joey' No very high awards, but it has made the judges look silly by its outstanding performance in the garden. The large, soft coppery orange blooms open with attractively waved petals and are carried without pause throughout the summer. The bush is of average height with dark, matt green leaves.

Free-flowering H.T. 'Just Joey'.

'National Trust' A fine rose that would be more popular if only it had some scent. It produces an unending succession of fairly small but very shapely, bright red blooms that stand up to rain well. A little below average height with matt, dark green leaves. RNRS Trial Ground Certificate.

'Paul Shirville' Started life quietly with a medal for fragrance and not much else but, as sometimes happens, its tremendous qualities have emerged in the garden. On the tall side at 90cm (3ft), it bears the most lovely salmon-pink flowers with peach-pink shadings. Leafy and spreading and a good cut flower.

'Peace' Almost too well-known to need description, but a 'must' in any list of the best. Very vigorous and bearing huge, soft yellow flowers with a pink flush on the petals' edges. Has been awarded Gold Medals galore during its long career.

Rainproof H.T. 'National Trust'.

Vigorous H.T. 'Peace'.

'Peaudouce' Has creamy primrose flowers of classic, high-centred shape on a bushy, 90cm (3ft) plant with plentiful, healthy mid- to dark green leaves. The scent is only moderate but its colour makes this a rose to soothe the spirit. RNRS Certificate of Merit.

'Piccadilly' A real old-timer from 1959 but still unsurpassed in its colour range – a bicolour, the scarlet petals having a yellow reverse. The moderately full blooms are carried with great freedom on a medium-sized, upright bush. Watch the glossy leaves for blackspot.

'Polar Star' The best pure white rose for many years, vigorous and tall, up to 1m (3½ft), it carries its shapely blooms singly and in clusters and is well branched and bushy. Rose of the Year for 1985.

'Precious Platinum' A misleading name for this is a bright red rose, the petals of which have a sheen that catches the eye. Good for cutting and at 75cm (2½ft) outstanding for bedding, its glossy leaves showing off the blooms well.

Hybrid tea 'Silver Jubilee'.

Hybrid tea 'Pink Favourite'.

'Pink Favourite' Would be included if for no other reason than its outstanding health. A strong grower to 90cm (3ft) with shapely, high-centred blooms in bright rose-pink but little scent. Needs some disbudding if it is to be seen at its best. RHS Award of Merit.

'Silver Jubilee' A RNRS President's International Trophy, the highest award of all, was well earned by this outstanding rose. The shapely flowers, of medium size unless some disbudding is done, are in blends of peach-pink and coppery, creamy pink. The glossy foliage is extremely healthy and covers the bushy plant right to the ground. Good for cutting if you are prepared to handle an excess of thorns!

Floribunda 'Amber Queen', an excellent bedding rose.

FLORIBUNDAS
'Amber Queen' This makes a marvellous bedding rose, the cupped, amber-yellow flowers, which are carried with incredible profusion and continuity, highlighted against the dark green, glossy leaves. The Rose of the Year in 1984 and a Certificate of Merit award.

'Anne Harkness' A rose that grows to 1m (3½ft) and needs quite hard pruning to keep it from becoming top heavy. But its height makes for long stems when its huge trusses of double apricot-orange are used as cut flowers. In water it will last and last, in the house or on the show bench. It flowers rather late – right through August – when many other notable roses are resting.

Floribunda 'Anne Harkness'.

'Arthur Bell' A Certificate of Merit in 1964 heralded what was to prove one of the best yellow Floribundas. The flowers are large, opening flat and paling somewhat with age. They come in medium-sized trusses on a tall plant with very healthy and glossy, leathery leaves. The fragrance is particularly outstanding. Certificate of Merit.

'Champagne Cocktail' Received a special award for the best rose raised by an amateur in 1985 and a Trial Ground Certificate. It is strongly scented, the trusses of flowers pale yellow, splashed and flecked with carmine; quite unique. Free-flowering, bushy to medium height and generally healthy.

'City of Belfast' For a number of years now this Gold Medal rose has been one of the best medium- to low-growing, scarlet bedding roses. The blooms are not large but make up for this in sheer quantity. Health is well up to average but there is little scent.

'City of Leeds' Leeds, too, did well with the rose named after it. Large clusters of moderately full blooms in salmon-pink carried with great freedom. Good for cutting and exhibition as it lasts in water. Growth bushy and height medium; no scent. It was awarded a Gold Medal when first introduced.

'Dame of Sark' Good for a large bed or low hedge as it will reach 1m (3½ft) and has the most striking clusters of flowers in bright orange-red with a yellow base to the petals and a yellow reverse. These have very little scent but the colour compensates and the very good mid-green, glossy leaves have a good health record. Trial Ground Certificate.

'City of Belfast', floribunda.

'City of Leeds', floribunda.

'Elizabeth of Glamis' Those with heavy, cold soils will not thank me for including this one, but if you have a light soil do not miss this lovely, scented rose. The soft salmon-orange blooms are shapely in the bud but open flat and are carried in medium-sized trusses. Probably not the healthiest of roses, even on dry soils, but nothing that spraying will not control. Gold Medal and Award of Merit, so I am not alone in rooting for this one, despite it having a few weaknesses.

'English Miss' Clusters of light rose-pink, double blooms on an upright bush of medium height or a little less. Very dark leaves set the flowers off to good advantage. A good scent and a Trial Ground Certificate.

'Escapade' Something really different, for the large flowers – carried on good-sized trusses – are rosy violet, paling to white in the centre; a most pleasing combination. Of medium height, the plant is a bushy one with light green, glossy leaves and a good health record. Good as a cut flower. Certificate of Merit.

'Evelyn Fison' Like 'City of Belfast', a fine scarlet bedding rose but a rather taller one. The colour is quite unfading even in the hottest sun and growth is bushy with rather small leaves on which blackspot is possible. Lasts when cut. A Gold Medal rose.

'Eye Paint' Though classed as a Floribunda, at 90cm–1.2m (3–4ft) in height this could be called a shrub rose. Very bushy and well branched, it has a good covering of dark green, semi-glossy leaves with clusters of flowers in great profusion all over the bush. They are small, single, and of the brightest scarlet with a white eye and reverse to the petals. Very striking when grown as a hedge.

The floribunda 'Escapade'.

'Eye Paint', tall floribunda.

'Fragrant Delight', a first-rate bedding floribunda.

'Iceberg', vigorous floribunda.

The floribunda 'Korresia'.

'Fragrant Delight' A little above average height, this makes a first-rate bedding rose with the bonus of a sweet scent. The flowers, shapely in the bud, open more loosely, and are of a coppery salmon with yellow shadings. The leaves are bronze-tinted when young, becoming a glossy dark green. A medal for fragrance and a Trial Ground Certificate.

'Iceberg' For long everybody's favourite, this wonderful white rose is still a winner. Making a shrub if pruned lightly, it carries its white flowers at all levels on a graceful, airy bush. Gold Medal.

'Korresia' One of the best yellow Floribundas of recent years, tough, reliable and healthy, with large clusters of fragrant yellow blooms on a bushy plant of medium height with a good covering of glossy, mid-green leaves.

'Lilli Marlene' has for long been a favourite floribunda.

'Lilli Marlene' Plum-red shoots and dark green leaves blend with the dusky scarlet flowers. The blooms come in good-sized clusters and hold well, though very hot sun can scorch the petal edges. Of medium height, this is a long-time favourite with a Gold Medal and Award of Merit to its name.

'Living Fire' After more than ten years, only just beginning to be recognized as the good rose it is. Quite large blooms in well-spaced trusses with good rain resistance and continuity. Healthy dark green leaves on a plant that is medium to tall. Colour: orange-scarlet with touches of yellow.

'Margaret Merril' Large white flowers with just a hint of the palest pink and pink stamens, the most lovely combination, especially when coupled with a sweet fragrance. A sturdy, bushy plant of medium height and dark green, glossy leaves, not immune to blackspot. Awarded a Certificate of Merit.

The floribunda 'Matangi'.

'Matangi' Perhaps the best of the so-called 'hand-painted' roses of Sam McGredy, and certainly the healthiest. The flowers, in large trusses, are orange-vermilion shading into a silvery eye with a silvery reverse to the petals. Bushy in form and of medium height. Gold Medal.

'Memento' A rose that won higher awards abroad than in the United Kingdom and deserved every one of them. Throughout the summer it is seldom, if ever, without a fine show of bright, cherry-red flowers. These are quite undismayed by bad weather, an enormous asset in a bedding rose. The glossy leaves are bronze-tinted when young on a bushy plant that will reach 75cm (2½ft).

'News' A difficult rose to describe as its colour is unlike any other. Its raiser's 'beetroot purple' is as near as one can get for the large flowers, which have golden stamens. Vigorous and compact to average height, it may need watching for blackspot. RNRS Gold Medal.

'Pink Parfait' The flowers at first are like those of miniature Hybrid Teas but later open wide. The trusses vary from medium to large, the blooms being a combination of light pink and creamy yellow. Tall and freely branching, this one will top 90cm (3ft) and makes a good hedge. Practically thornless and a Gold Medal winner.

'News', unusual floribunda.

Floribunda 'Pink Parfait' is practically thornless.

'Queen Elizabeth' Large, cupped flowers in bright rose-pink that last for ever in the house but have little scent. An enormously tall and vigorous grower which, as it can top 2.4m (8ft) if lightly pruned, is for a hedge or the back of the border. Few thorns and very healthy leaves. RNRS Gold Medal.

'Southampton' A rose with cupped flowers almost the size of those of a Hybrid Tea early on, when they can be carried one to a stem. Later, in trusses, they are smaller and aptly described as being the colour of marmalade. Weather resistance first rate as is the late season flowering. A strong grower to 90cm (3ft) with very healthy, dark green leaves. Trial Ground Certificate but deserved better recognition.

'Sunsilk' Another Floribunda with Hybrid Tea-sized flowers, full and nicely shaped, in medium-sized clusters. The soft lemon-yellow can fade a little but is always pleasing. At a vigorous 75cm (2½ft) it is a good bedding rose. Trial Ground Certificate.

'The Times' Full, many-petalled flowers of a glowing, deep crimson, make this an outstanding new rose, especially when coupled with its deep green, red-tinted foliage that is exceptionally healthy. From 75–90cm (2½-3ft) in height, the plant is bushy and spreading. It won the RNRS President's International Trophy and you cannot do better than that!

'Wishing' A short grower to about 60cm (2ft) of a type now known as Patio Roses; bushy, compact and suitable for the smallest space – on a par with the larger miniatures. A wealth of peachy pink bloom of immaculate shape and a fine health record make this one of the newer roses with a great future. Awarded a well-deserved Certificate of Merit.

The floribunda 'Southampton'.

Floribunda 'The Times'.

CLIMBERS AND RAMBLERS

'Compassion' The shapely, sweetly-scented blooms of this rose are in blends of pink and apricot and as it is fully recurrent, come with the greatest freedom throughout the summer. The dark green leaves are healthy and this is a strong recommendation for a climber that will reach about 3m (10ft) and can be relied upon to cover a wall well with its many-branched canes.

'Golden Showers' Not quite so vigorous as 'Compassion' but bearing just as many flowers, this time in bright yellow. Shapely at first, they open loosely and can fade a little, but do not mind rain. The canes are almost thornless and carry healthy, glossy, dark green leaves. Can make a fine free-standing shrub.

'Handel' This one will reach 4.5m (15ft) and has bronze-tinted deep green leaves that may need watching for disease. The trusses of flowers are very freely borne and each bloom is creamy white, the petal edges rosy pink, a colour that gradually suffuses the whole flower. Trial Ground Certificate.

'New Dawn' One of the most popular climbing roses and still going from strength to strength after nearly sixty years, both in gardens and as a parent of other new varieties. The soft pink flowers are carried in tremendous profusion in early summer and continuity thereafter is good. A sweet scent and mid-green leaves not immune to mildew.

Climber 'Golden Showers'.

'Handel', a climber.

'Swan Lake' is a strong-growing climber for a large wall.

'Pink Perpetue' More constantly in flower than almost any other climber and one of the few that puts on as good a show in the autumn as it does in its first June flush if a little deadheading is done. The blooms come in large clusters but are not particularly big in themselves. However, they are fully double, rose-pink with a carmine reverse. Not much scent. Good for a pillar, fence or low wall. Certificate of Merit.

'Swan Lake' A strong grower that will cover a large wall and has very large, shapely blooms, white with a hint of pink. Considering the number of petals in each, weather resistance is exceptionally good, but there is little scent. The glossy leaves may need watching for blackspot late in the season.

'Albéric Barbier' One of the healthiest of ramblers and almost ever-green, with dark, glossy leaves and a vigour that will take it to 4.5m (15ft) or more. The fragrant flowers, in small clusters, open from orange-yellow buds to a creamy white.

'Félicité et Perpétue' Taking us back to the early 1800s, this one has survived because of the unbelievable profusion of its many-petalled, pompon-style white blooms, which open from pink-tinted buds. Such a display makes up for the fact that it is not recurrent. The dark green, glossy leaves stay on the plant most of the winter. Up to 4.5m (15ft) and many-branched.

'François Juranville' From the same stable as the ever popular 'Albertine' and just as good. Very double flowers that open flat and are filled with coral-pink petals. The flowering period is exceptionally long but there is no repeat.

MINIATURES

'Bit o' Sunshine' This is one of the bigger miniatures, which means that it will reach 38cm (15in) or so. The light yellow blooms, which are large and very full, may fade slightly, but they are quite well scented for a miniature, a group not noted for perfume. Some protection from blackspot and mildew may be needed for this one.

'Baby Masquerade' The flowers of this variety change colour in just the same way as the Floribunda from which it gets its name. In other words, they move from yellow to pink to a deeper red, though the red is a more pleasing tone than that of the larger rose. A fine, bushy grower that will reach 38cm (15in) but keeps the small flowers and leaves of the true miniature. As healthy as most of these small plants.

'Darling Flame' In any popularity poll of miniatures this would come near, if not at, the top, as it is one of the best introductions of recent years. The flowers are carried with great freedom on a bushy plant and are double and a glowing orange-vermilion with a yellow petal reverse. Up to about 30cm (1ft).

Miniature 'Darling Flame'.

Miniature 'Baby Masquerade' – the flowers change colour.

The flowers of miniature 'Starina' last well when cut.

'Fire Princess' As it reaches 45cm (1½ft) it could be argued that this should not be called a miniature, but it is a miniature in most other ways. The small, slightly scented double blooms are bright scarlet and last well when cut. Good for showing.

'Gypsy Jewel' Has most pleasing, double, rose-pink blooms in clusters on a 30cm (1ft) plant that tends to sprawl a little but it is reasonably bushy as it branches well. A good health record and a colour not found too often in the miniature range.

'Red Ace' Miniature roses are appearing more and more frequently on the show bench, not only at national shows but at local ones as well. They are certainly easier to transport than the full-size roses, but put on a remarkable display despite their size. In this, 'Red Ace' is invariably to the fore with dark crimson blooms on a compact, upright plant of medium height.

'Snow Carpet' Something quite different as this is a ground cover rose and one that really does hug the ground, covering about a square yard. The blooms are white, double, and carried freely. Growth is bushy and sprawling, no more than 7.5–10cm (3–4in) high. Keeps down weeds. Trial Ground Certificate.

'Starina' Its glowing orange-vermilion double flowers are among the most long-lasting when cut. They come in great profusion on a 45cm (1½ft) plant.

'Stars 'n' Stripes' A novelty in that the white flowers are striped and splashed red. They are large and semi-double, opening loosely but very showy. Growth is lax but it will reach 30cm (1ft). No scent.

SHRUB ROSES OLD AND NEW

'Aloha' A modern shrub with the most sumptuous double, old-style flowers in warm rose-pink. Sweetly scented, they are practically rain-proof and the shiny foliage will rarely if ever be troubled by disease. A sturdy, upright grower to about 1.2m (4ft), it will also climb, though slowly, if it is planted near a wall. Recurrent flowers.

'Buff Beauty' One of the Hybrid Musk group of roses which are re-nowned for their massed display of flowers. In 'Buff Beauty' they are a warm orange-buff and will repeat well with the help of a little dead-heading. The plant, with healthy, dark green leaves, tends to sprawl and may need some support.

'Canary Bird' A species or near relative of one, though no-one is quite certain of its origin. Long, arching canes carrying all along their length in May and early June bright yellow single flowers with great freedom. Will reach a height and spread of 1.8 x 2.1m (6 x 7ft) and has attractive, ferny foliage.

Shrub rose 'Canary Bird'.

Sweetly scented modern shrub rose 'Aloha'.

45

'Fantin Latour' From the old Centifolia family, this makes a big, 1.8m (6ft) shrub, its shoots weighed down in early summer with clusters of very double blooms of the palest blush-pink. No repeat, of course, with this ancient family, but the large, dark green leaves are an attraction after the flowers are over, provided a watch is kept for mildew. This is one of the most beautiful of the old roses.

'Felicia' Another Hybrid Musk and a more upright grower than 'Buff Beauty'. Just as many flowers, however, if not more and in larger trusses. They are double and a warm pink, with a good scent. Some deadheading is needed to encourage the second crop. Felicia will make a bushy, 1.5m (5ft) shrub, with about roughly the same spread.

'Golden Wings' A fairly modern rose that looks like a species with its large, single, soft yellow flowers, but they are produced non-stop right through the summer. A healthy, 1.5m (5ft) bush with mid-green leaves. The flowers are sweetly scented and have amber stamens. RHS Award of Merit.

The shrub rose 'Golden Wings'.

Centifolia shrub 'Fantin Latour' makes a large specimen.

The old gallica, 'Rosa Mundi', makes a fine show in mid-summer.

'Rosa Mundi' This one comes from the oldest rose family, the Gallicas, and dates back to the sixteenth century at least. A twiggy, bushy shrub about 1.2m (4ft) tall, at mid-summer it carries the gayest of flowers: white, striped and splashed pink. They open with attractively waved petals and make a great show. However, the foliage will have to be watched for mildew after the flowers have gone.

'Roseraie de l'Hay' Of the Rugosa family and hence bearing the typical crinkled or rugose foliage, which is practically disease-proof. As the leaf coverage goes right to the ground, this rose forms a fine hedge, its prickly stems making it a formidable barrier. Double, wine-red flowers with the sweetest scent are carried continuously throughout the summer and on into the autumn.

Shrub rose 'Sally Holmes'.

'Sally Holmes' Raised by an amateur, this makes a wide, bushy shrub of about 1.2m (4ft) with beautiful, dark green leaves. They set off well the large, single, soft pink flowers which soon fade to a delightful creamy white. The repeat is also first rate.

INDEX AND ACKNOWLEDGEMENTS

Picture credits

Pat Brindley: 1, 6(t,b), 7(r), 8(t,b), 11(b), 13, 31, 32(t,b), 34(b), 35(t),
37(bl,br), 38(t), 39(t,b), 43(t,b), 45(b), 46(t,b), 47(b).
Michael Gibson: 7(l), 30(b), 33(l), 40(l).
John Glover: 12(b). Lyn and Derek Gould: 36(r).
ICI: 26(tl,b). S & O Mathews: 27(bl).
Harry Smith Horticultural Photographic Collection: 28/9.
Michael Warren: 4/5, 9(t,b), 10, 11(t), 12(t), 22, 23(t,b), 26(tr), 27(br),
30(t), 32(br), 33(r), 34(t), 35(b), 36(l), 37(t), 38(b), 40(r), 41(b), 42,
44, 45(t), 47(t).

Artwork by Simon Roulstone